D1712981

SEAN "DIDDY" COMBS

A Biography of a Music Mogul

Jen Jones

Enslow Publishers, Inc.
40 Industrial Road
Box 398
Berkeley Heights, NJ 07922
USA

http://www.enslow.com

Library of Congress Cataloging-in-Publication Data
Jones, Jen.
    Sean "Diddy" Combs : a biography of a music mogul / Jen Jones.
        pages cm. — (African-American icons)
    Includes bibliographical references, discography, and index.
    Summary: "Explores the life of music mogul Sean "Diddy" Combs, including his child-hood, his ascent to fame in the music industry, his family life, and his great success as an entrepreneur"—Provided by publisher.
    ISBN 978-0-7660-4296-4
    1. Diddy, 1969—Juvenile literature. 2. Rap musicians—United States—Biography—Juvenile literature. I. Title.
    ML3930.P84J66 2014
    782.421649092—dc23
    [B]
                            2013009372

Future editions:
Paperback ISBN: 978-1-4644-0537-2
EPUB ISBN: 978-1-4645-1274-2
Single-User PDF ISBN: 978-1-4646-1274-9
Multi-User PDF ISBN: 978-0-7660-5906-1

Printed in the United States of America
112013 Lake Book Manufacturing, Inc., Melrose Park, IL
10 9 8 7 6 5 4 3 2 1

To Our Readers:
We have done our best to make sure all Internet addresses in this book were active and appropriate when we went to press. However, the author and the publisher have no control over and assume no liability for the material available on those Internet sites or on other Web sites they may link to. Any comments or suggestions can be sent by e-mail to comments@enslow.com or to the address on the back cover.

✪ Enslow Publishers, Inc., is committed to printing our books on recycled paper. The paper in every book contains 10% to 30% post-consumer waste (PCW). The cover board on the outside of each book contains 100% PCW. Our goal is to do our part to help young people and the environment too!

Cover Illustration: AP Images / Dan Steinberg

CONTENTS

Chapter 1

THE FATHER OF REINVENTION

The sound of violins, drums, and cellos filled Los Angeles' Nokia Theatre as a full orchestra played the intro to "Coming Home" on its stage. A giant puff of smoke took over the room. When it disappeared, in its place was Sean John Combs— better known to the 2010 American Music Awards audience as simply "Diddy." With this performance, Combs was debuting a new model of his image: Diddy-Dirty Money. Always one to make a big entrance, Combs gave a rousing rendition of his hit song. Fans waved their hands back and forth in support. His son smiled in the audience. Fireworks went off in the background, signaling that his new group was more than ready to make a splash.

For Combs, it was the start of yet another chapter in what had already been a long career. It's not surprising that fans were willing to embrace his new approach. After all, anyone who follows Combs knows that he's constantly evolving. For this busy music mogul, identity has meant everything. He's got the collection of names to prove it.

He'd grown up as "Puff," a streetwise high school football player known for huffing and puffing when he didn't get his way. During his time at Howard University, he'd morphed into "Puffy," an ambitious intern-turned-executive determined to conquer the music business. And with the 1997 release of his multiplatinum debut album *No Way Out*, Combs became "Puff Daddy," a larger-than-life rap artist and CEO known for flaunting his love of the good life. Though by that point he was a household name, not everyone always "got" it. At one event, former Secretary of State Henry Kissinger mused, "Why does he call himself Fluffy?"

Image and identity have played a big part in propelling Combs through two decades of stardom, heartbreak, and scandal. He had a long climb to the top of the entertainment industry from humble beginnings in Harlem. From "Puff Daddy" to "King Combs" to "Swag," Combs is always finding new ways—and names—to reinvent his legacy.

Flash back to 2001, when the power of this approach became clear. Having successfully made the switch from music executive to platinum-selling recording artist, Combs should have been on top of the world. Yet Combs was tempted to disappear from the public eye. He wanted to take a break from the celebrity status he'd worked so hard to create.

His position was understandable. In 1997, his close friend, Christopher "Notorious B.I.G." Wallace, had been gunned down while Combs watched. In a separate incident, Combs had been accused of shooting a gun in a nightclub. As a result, he had weathered a high-stress trial—breaking up with girlfriend Jennifer Lopez in the process. After hitting a high point with artists like Wallace in the 1990s, his music label, Bad Boy, was in a state of change. Sales were declining and artists jumped ship. *Forever,* the follow-up to his smash debut, struggled on the music charts.

On top of it all, Combs was fed up with the media criticizing his every move. "There has been so much overshadowing my music," Combs told *Ebony* in 2000. "One week you'll hear that I'm messing with this girl; the next week, you'll hear that I made this amount of money; the next week, you'll hear that I was hanging out with Donald Trump. A lot of times, the music gets lost. But that's all I'm trying to do: make music. That's what 'Puff Daddy' is all about."

The once promising future seemed grim. "How do you go from being king of the world to hanging over the rails in two short years?" asked the *Washington Post* in December 1999 of Combs's seeming fall from favor.

Combs was left to figure it out. "I don't have all the answers," Combs said at the time. "I'm taking time off to try to get answers for myself—Sean Combs—to take some time out for me, to take a break from this celebrityism. Just evaluate myself as a person."

It was time for the self-proclaimed "bad boy" to start over.

After briefly stepping out of the spotlight, Combs reemerged as "P. Diddy" in 2001—once again ready to take on the world. It was later in 2005 that he shortened his nickname to just "Diddy." "It was something I was doing for myself personally, just like I always change my credits," Combs told *Jet* in 2001. "It's just something creatively I do and I thought it was time for a fresh start."

Since recommitting to his passion, he hasn't stopped. As the resident hit maker and CEO of Bad Boy Entertainment, Combs has reignited the label by signing successful artists, such as Yung Joc, Danity Kane, Machine Gun Kelly, and Cassie. He continues to release his own hit albums, too. Combs has also diversified his efforts. Far from just a music man, he has found success in the fields of fashion, entrepreneurship, film/television production, and philanthropy. On any given day, Combs might be producing an MTV reality show, walking a red carpet, running a fashion show for his Sean John clothing line, or making an endorsement deal with a major brand.

Undoubtedly, the hard work has paid off. In 2012, *Forbes* magazine deemed Combs the wealthiest artist in hip-hop with a net worth of $550 million. It's likely that one of Combs's favorite mottoes, "Sleeping Is for Losers," is in play in order for him to make it all happen. After all, Combs is willing to do whatever it takes to stay at the top.

"When young people look at me, I want them to not just look at me as an American dream—I want them to look at me as an American reality," Combs said to CNBC in 2007. "This is what you get through hard work and perseverance. I feel like the true champions work the hardest, whether it's Michael Jordan staying in the gym to do a hundred thousand free throws or Tiger Woods starting at the age of six.

When you look at the great ones . . . they all have that in common—they work hard."

Still on Combs's to-do list? "I think I'm going to become a big Hollywood star," Combs told CNBC in the same interview. "I think I'll go tackle the big screen."

The lofty goal is no surprise in light of Combs's habit of reinvention. With a trio of impressive movie roles already, he's well on his way to making it happen. His acting name of choice? Simply "Sean Combs."

"I've always been fascinated with the art of storytelling," Combs told James Lipton on an episode of *Inside the Actor's Studio*. "[If] you listen to my music as a producer, it's very cinematic. Interludes, movie-type of scores were always things I intertwined into my music, [along with] a plot, stories and different acts."

In 2001, Combs appeared in the movie *Made* alongside Vince Vaughn and Jon Favreau, opening the door to future opportunities. He began getting offers to appear in what he viewed as typical rapper roles. But Combs was more interested in doing something raw and independent. When he heard about the film *Monster's Ball* starring Halle Berry and Billy Bob Thornton, Combs immediately knew that was the right role to jump-start a serious acting career.

Combs began working with acting coach Susan Batson to prepare for the audition. However, he was later told they weren't interested in auditioning him for the part. Combs was discouraged, but Batson told him not to take no for an answer. "They have this stereotype of you," she told him. "If I was you, I would jump on your jet and tell Halle Berry and Lee Daniels that you want this role."[1]

The next day, Combs did just that and found himself knocking on Berry's hotel room door—asking for "just five minutes" of her time. "[I said,] 'Do you remember when people looked at you as just a pretty face and no one would give you that chance?'" Combs said. The next day, he landed the audition—and the part of Lawrence Musgrove, a prisoner on death row. The film was highly acclaimed, winning Halle Berry a Best Actress Oscar and also winning an Academy Award for Best Screenplay.

Not many fledgling actors start out in an Oscar-nominated film, but Combs wasn't done yet. In 2004, Combs turned his attention to the Broadway stage. He took the lead role in a revival of *A Raisin in the Sun*. Based on the Langston Hughes poem "Harlem" and the play by Lorraine Hansberry, the powerful stage production chronicled the experiences of a struggling African-American family in Chicago. Combs starred alongside respected actresses Audra

McDonald, Phylicia Rashad, and Sanaa Lathan. He took a chance on acting in front of a live audience.

"It was definitely scary when the opportunity presented itself, but I didn't hesitate to jump at the chance, and I've stuck in there," Combs told *Playbill* in 2004. "I think it was something that said to me, 'By God, as an actor, this is the chance of a lifetime!'"

By many accounts, it was. The show was one of few profitable shows on Broadway that year, boasting more than $700,000 worth of box-office returns. Combs was hailed as a "Broadway rainmaker." He made such an impression that he was later cast alongside the other original stars for the television movie adaptation. It was later nominated for an Emmy award for Outstanding Made for Television Movie. The movie was the first of several television stints for Combs, who later made appearances on such shows as *Hawaii Five-O* and *CSI: Miami*.

In 2010, Combs costarred in the Judd Apatow-directed comedy *Get Him to the Greek* as over-the-top music executive "Sergio Roma." Combs later described the character as "tri-polar, so fun and so crazy." Faced with his first comedic feature film, Combs relied on his natural sense of humor and improvisation instincts to find his way. "Everything you see me say in the film is coming off the top of my head," he said. "I'm best when I have no restrictions."

Though many novice actors would have been intimidated to take the screen alongside such seasoned comedians as Russell Brand and Jonah Hill, Combs saw no other option but to hold his own. "To play at that level of the game, you've got to be funny; if you're not naturally funny, there's no way," Combs told *Playboy* in 2009. "That's like throwing the ball around with Michael Jordan and LeBron James."

Whether it's trying on a new name or playing a new role, it's clear Combs is here to stay. "Through all the wars, the ups and downs, the cold times, the hot times, the rumors, the shiny suits, whatever—all that—[I'm] still standing," he told *Vibe* in 2006. "I represent success, aspiration, lifestyle and the entrepreneurial spirit. I am that American dream. I come from Harlem, New York, humble beginnings. I always wanted something more."[2]

Chapter 2

GROWING UP DIDDY

Much like music legends Alicia Keys and Tupac Shakur, Sean "Diddy" Combs hails from New York City's Harlem district. Over the years, Harlem has spawned many success stories, as it's known for bringing fame to many entertainers through the popular "Showtime at the Apollo" at its Apollo Theater. A largely African-American neighborhood, 1960s Harlem was considered a dangerous "ghetto" rife with drug use, crime, poverty, and racial tension. Though many of its residents lived in low-income housing projects, Sean grew up in a middle-class apartment building known as Esplanade Gardens.

Sean was born to parents Melvin and Janice Combs on November 4, 1969. His sister, Keisha, was born in 1971. Melvin was a cab driver and former Board of Education worker, while Janice was a working model. She often wore furs around the house, which shaped young Sean's view of fashion. "[My mom] was always like the fly girl of the neighborhood, and my pops was the fly guy of the neighborhood," Sean has said. "That's what attracted them. That's how they got together."[1]

Life took a tragic turn for the Combs family in 1972, when Melvin was shot in the head and killed in Central Park. Without Janice's knowledge, Melvin had started dealing drugs and had fallen into the wrong crowd. Though Melvin had bought the family an expensive Mercedes, Janice later told author Ronin Ro that she never had any reason to suspect illegal activity. "I never knew about the drugs stuff because he always worked; he did it in between times."

At the time, Sean knew nothing of the real reason his father was killed. Janice protected her children by telling them Melvin was killed in a car accident. "My mother didn't want me to follow in his footsteps, so she was selective about which truths she told me," Sean said in a 2006 interview with Oprah Winfrey. "[She said] my father was in the army and he owned a limousine service, and he died in a car accident."

It wasn't until Sean was fourteen years old that he decided to dig deeper and learned that his father had been a drug dealer. On a trip to the library, Sean searched for Melvin's name in the microfilm archives. "[I found out] they had called him a 'kingpin' . . . in Harlem, and that he was killed in Central Park West," Sean told James Lipton during an *Inside the Actor's Studio* appearance in 2010.

Childhood memories came flooding back as Sean started to piece together what had really happened. "[As a kid], I noticed that guys from the streets in Harlem always seemed to know my family's last name," Sean said. "'I used to run with your father,' they'd told me. All my uncles were street hustlers as well."

Looking back, Sean is understanding of his father's choice. "During that time, that was the only way out of Harlem—that or playing basketball," he told Oprah in 2006.

Sean's only wish? That he had more memories of Melvin. Sean's recollection of his father is blurry since he was only three at the time of his father's death. "I would dream about him throwing me up in the air," Sean told Lipton. "That's the only memory I have of him."

Suddenly a single mother, Janice was placed in the difficult position of supporting a family of three.

Though it would have been tempting to move the family to give them a fresh start, Janice opted to stay in Harlem, taking a variety of jobs. Her work duties ranged from helping kids with cerebral palsy to driving a school bus to working at a baby boutique to cocktail waitressing at an "after-hours spot" for big tips. As Janice told Lipton on *Inside the Actor's Studio*, her motivation was keeping the family close to its roots. "I wanted them to have the experience of Harlem and to be around their culture, and I figured that this was the best place for them to have this education," she explained.

While juggling several jobs, Janice saved up money for a house and tried to give her children the best opportunities possible. When Sean was eight years old, she enrolled him in a Fresh Air Fund camp that sent him to Pennsylvania to live with an Amish family for the summer. "It was a culture shock. I got time to walk around and think and relax," Sean remembers. "I got to see different people and be open-minded to different things instead of just the environment I was in. That's what helped make me what I am today."[2]

Later in life, the experience inspired Sean to found Daddy's House Social Programs, which hosts an annual sleepaway camp in various locations.

Around this time, Sean also began honing his street smarts. Once back in Harlem, he started getting into scuffles—one in which he was beaten up and had his skateboard stolen. When Sean told Janice about the incident, she told him not to return until he had recovered it.

"Outside, [Combs] ran into a taller, older kid and asked him to handle the job," writes Ronin Ro in *Bad Boy: The Influence of Sean "Puffy" Combs on the Music Industry*. "Thus began his habit of forging alliances with tougher kids." Mission accomplished—Sean had a newfound outlook *and* his skateboard back.

A similar event took place when nine-year-old Sean went to the store to buy something for his grandmother, and his money was stolen. Sean went home crying to his mother, who told him, "Go back out there and get that money, and if anyone ever puts their hands on you, make sure they never do it again," Sean later told Oprah. "She knew the reality—if people smell weakness, they take advantage of you. You have to defend yourself."

The encounters personified what life was like in Harlem on a daily basis—not only for Sean, but for many that resided there. "In Harlem, it's very tense. You have your guard on—it's like a warzone," he said in a 2003 *NY1.com* interview. "It's definitely a different mentality."

In 1982, Janice decided to move the family to safer, more family-friendly surroundings. The Combs family relocated to suburban Mount Vernon, New York, in nearby Westchester County. She enrolled twelve-year-old Sean in highly regarded Mount Vernon Montessori School. He took on multiple paper routes to help foot the higher cost of living. Sean was comforted by the serenity of his new surroundings: "I remember the simple things about Mount Vernon: grass, trees and being able to play baseball. In Harlem, there was no Little League, no front yard with grass."[3]

Sean went on to attend a private all-boys high school, Mount Saint Michael Academy in the Bronx, where a sign inside the door reads "The City Streets Stop Here." His experience there played a large role in shaping the "Puffy" rap fans now know and love. Tall and athletic, Sean ran track and joined the football team, on which he played cornerback and running back. Though Sean has always been mum on the exact origin of his now-famous nickname, many accounts say he earned the name "Puffy" for his tendency to puff out his chest to make his body seem bigger.

Along with his alter ego, Sean's love for music and rap culture also started to take shape. He shaved musical notes into his "Gumby" hairstyle, a then-popular type of Afro. When not wearing his school uniform, Sean would rock wild polka-dot shirts and other street-style apparel. His Walkman was loaded with hip-hop artists ranging from LL Cool J to Beastie Boys to KRS-One. At night, he would sneak out to see live performances.

"I'd be out until three, four in the morning, seeing the music. I had to sneak out to do it, but I was doing it," Sean confessed.[4] After school, he'd hang out back in Harlem, getting to know up-and-coming artists.

Shades of Sean's entrepreneurial side also emerged. Every day, he'd pocket and save the lunch money Janice gave him, as well as "ask everybody for fifty cents" that he saw in the cafeteria. Though it's unknown how much he saved, Sean was getting good practice honing his powers of persuasion. It was more than just a game for Sean, though—it was important that he help defer the costs of his schooling. Along with his existing paper routes, he took a job working at a Rye, New York-based amusement park, Playland Park. Many years later, the video for Mariah Carey's No. 1 single "Fantasy," featuring and produced by Combs, would be shot there.

Though some of his classmates mocked him for having to work double shifts to get by, Sean was undeterred. "Like a lot of kids who grow up in single-parent homes, I had to get a job much quicker and start thinking about the future much earlier. I had to help out and become the man of the house," he told the *Black Collegian* in 2005. "I used to always get cracked on by the other kids [for] having two and three jobs, but I would always say to myself that I wanted to be somebody who makes history."

Though Sean clearly had a passion for hip-hop, he didn't have plans on pursuing it as a career yet. In 1986, the Mount Saint Michael Mountaineers won a division title, and he set his sights on becoming a professional football player. "There's nothing that you could tell me, that I wasn't gonna be playing in the NFL," Combs told Lipton on *Inside the Actors' Studio*. In true Combs style, he tweeted years later that his goal was to become the first African-American majority owner of an NFL football team.

Yet life intervened his senior year of high school, halting Sean's path toward professional football. On his last day of training camp before the football season began, Sean broke his leg and had to sit out the season. Heartbroken, Sean had to start over from the sidelines and miss prime opportunities to be seen by talent scouts. "I had to learn at a young age that . . . things happen, and sometimes your dreams get deferred," Sean told Lipton. "That's when I found music."

In search of a new direction, Sean threw himself into the emerging hip-hop scene. Whenever possible, he snuck out of the house to mix with such rising stars as rap producer Teddy Riley and rapper Kool Moe Dee back in the city at The Rooftop nightclub. He also practiced his dance moves at the clubs and back home while listening to New York City R&B radio station WBLS-FM. Sean's confident swagger and smooth moves didn't go unnoticed. As a teenager, he appeared as a backup dancer in music videos for R&B singer Stacy Lattisaw, pop group Fine Young Cannibals, and rapper Doug E. Fresh.

Sean began to envision himself rising through the ranks of the music industry. He focused his energy on making his dream happen and taking the next step toward success. "Everybody has a dream when they're watching Run DMC or LL Cool J," Sean once stated. "They think, 'I wish I was that.' I was always somebody who closed my eyes and dreamed, but then opened my eyes and saw what I had to do."[5]

Chapter 3

HIP-HOP'S NEWEST BAD BOY

For Sean Combs, the road to becoming hip-hop's most highly paid artist began when he headed to Howard University as a freshman in 1988. From the moment Combs landed on the Washington, D.C., campus, he established himself as a mover and a shaker among the primarily black student body. Many of his peers even recognized him from music videos they'd seen on MTV or from modeling jobs he'd done for *Essence* and Baskin-Robbins as a young boy.

"When Puffy came, he was a very flashy guy," said friend and future business partner Deric Angelettie.

"He was always out at the clubs, and the young girls loved him. He'd be in the middle of the floor doin' all the new dances. And his style of dress was a little more colorful, bolder. Everyone took notice of this cool, overconfident young dude."[1]

While some may have gotten caught up in the party scene, Combs worked as hard as he played. As he later told the *Los Angeles Times,* the business administration major got his "entrepreneurial hustle on." He ran an airport shuttle service for students traveling home and sold T-shirts and sodas around campus. Combs even found a way to profit off a heated protest in which students stormed an administrative building on campus, gathering media clips and selling poster-sized collages to participants.

Yet Combs found the most success as a party promoter. His weekly hip-hop dance parties soon became the hottest ticket on campus, especially after Combs partnered with fellow Howard student and deejay Angelettie. The pair formed an event production company called "A Black Man and a Puerto Rican Productions," named in honor of their respective ethnicities. Their first joint party became legendary for attracting boldface names such as Heavy D, Slick Rick, Doug E. Fresh, and Guy. Combs had first approached fellow Mount Vernon native Heavy D about attending and then used his name to convince the other artists to attend. Larger than life in both personality and appearance, Heavy D was well-loved and respected in the rap community. "Since that first party, everyone made it a point to go to Puff's parties," colleague Ron Gilyard recalled.

Combs continued to partner with other business-savvy students. Their parties became so popular that even Howard University wanted a piece of the action. The university asked Combs's company to plan and promote some of its large-scale events for students and alumni. "Our biggest [event] was Homecoming '89 at the Masonic Temple," Angelettie later recalled to author Ronin Ro. "I expected maybe 1,500 [people]; 4,500 came. The D.C. police shut down the whole block and brought out the dogs. We had to get on our knees and beg them not to lock us up."

It seemed Combs had the Midas touch—the parties had established him as one of the most connected men at Howard. "I started gaining friends from [the parties]; I could get anything I wanted on campus," he told *Vibe* in 1993. "If I needed to get my car fixed, I knew where to go. If I needed the English paper, I knew who to go to. If I needed an exam . . . I knew how to get it."

Though Combs often took the easy way out back then, he also admitted that he could have done things differently. "I had a lot of immature ways about me.

I don't agree with all that stuff now. I had a lot of growing up to do."

However, having so many hookups did allow Combs to turn his attention to his main focus: the music business. His interest was particularly piqued by a promotional video for a music compilation called *Uptown's Kickin' It*. The upbeat video featured Uptown Entertainment CEO Andre Harrell dressed in dapper business attire, surrounded by record executives. Combs later credited this video with sparking his desire to pursue a career in music: "I wanted to be the guy sitting at the head of the table, pushing contracts aside after signing them."

Though Combs had become somewhat of a big fish on campus, he felt it was time to lay the groundwork back in New York City and mingle with music executives. He landed an interview for an internship with Def Jam honcho Lyor Cohen but wasn't hired. "I didn't get a callback. I had on a polka-dot shirt at the time. It wasn't hip-hop enough for them," Combs later said during a United Jewish Appeal dinner honoring Cohen.

Discouraged but not deterred, Combs realized he would have to tap into his growing network and work his existing connections. He approached Heavy D. The rising star had not only forged a successful rap career but had also become the vice president of

Artists & Repertoire (A&R) at Uptown Entertainment. Heavy D agreed to make an introduction to Harrell, whom Combs had previously admired in the video. After all, Heavy D could relate to Combs's plight. Def Jam's cofounder, Russell Simmons, had once refused to sign him—telling Harrell that "nobody wants to sign a fat rapper."

Combs was appreciative. "Heavy D is the person who gave me my first chance in the music industry," Combs later tweeted after Heavy D's death in 2011. "He got me my internship at Uptown. He believed when no one else did."

Though many perceive the music industry as glamorous, Combs's beginnings were anything but. On Wednesday nights, he took a four-hour train ride from Washington, D.C. to New York City. He spent Thursdays and Fridays working at Uptown. He performed tedious tasks, such as fetching coffee, washing cars, and delivering tapes. On Friday, he made sure to be back by midnight in order to host his parties. Harrell later recalled one incident in which he asked Combs to pick up a tape from another building. Combs returned within minutes, out of breath from running. When Harrell asked him what was wrong, Combs answered, "I ran."

Meanwhile, Combs was losing sight of his studies, paying students to take notes for him in class and getting permission from professors for his many absences. To Combs, the sacrifice was worth it. He had no problem doing whatever was necessary to pay his dues music-wise. "I drove Andre's car; if they needed something delivered, I would take a cab instead of the subway and pay for it out of my own pocket. I knew [Uptown] was the place to be."

Though he was at the bottom of the pecking order, Combs didn't see himself that way. A dutiful intern, he took lengthy notes and closely watched everything going on inside the company. Well dressed, he looked the part of someone successful. "Even at 19, Combs was natty: crisp polo shirts, khakis, tight coif," said writer and filmmaker Barry Michael Cooper in a 2001 interview. "I don't ever remember him wearing sneakers. What I can't forget is how he watched everything and everybody."

Another thing Cooper will never forget is a conversation between him and Combs that took place in 1990 in front of Uptown/MCA's headquarters. Cooper was hailing a cab, and Combs struck up a conversation by telling Cooper that they'd both grown up in Esplanade Gardens. When Cooper didn't believe him, Combs recalled a fire that had taken place in the building to prove that he was telling the truth.

"Combs smiled as my jaw dropped. Actually, it was not so much a smile as a sardonic look, fixed by high cheekbones, a ravenous overbite, and thickly arched eyebrows," Cooper recalled. "He left me with this as my cab pulled up: 'When you write your next movie, keep me in mind. My name is Sean, but they call me Puffy. And I'm gonna be a big star. Remember that.'"

Combs's cockiness surfaced again one day at the gym, when Harrell introduced him to Def Jam's Simmons. Combs bet Simmons $700 that he could stay on the Stairmaster longer, even though Simmons was in great shape and Combs had never been on a Stairmaster. Ninety minutes later, Combs collected his winnings. He later used them to make repairs on his car.

Risky moves like that and Combs's overall attitude that he was equal to his superiors paid off. Soon, Combs was whisked into Harrell's inner circle. "My mom was driving me crazy—Andre let me live at his house [in Closter, New Jersey]. Right before he moved out, I put a hole in the wall, which cost 30 grand to fix," Combs later told *New York* magazine in 1995. "Then he let me live at his house in Alpine. I mean I was 20 years old, living in a mansion with a . . . pool."

Cooper remembers dazzling nights in Manhattan at the Royalton Hotel. Harrell and friends sipped expensive champagne and talked about the art of being "ghetto fabulous." Observing it all with a careful eye, Cooper was struck by the way Combs soaked up the scene as Harrell commanded the room. Later, he wrote about the way Combs modeled his approach after his mentor and assumed "Harrell's energy."

Combs decided to convince Harrell to give him a full-time job and more responsibility. He took Harrell out to lunch with a simple pitch: "I am your demographic." Harrell bit, and Combs dropped out of Howard University to replace Kurt Woodley as Uptown's head of Artists & Repertoire (A&R). His new job would entail scouting talent and helping to nurture the label's existing artists.

Combs had already worked closely with a number of Uptown artists, including Rare Essence and Father MC. But his first real success was with hip-hop/R&B quartet Jodeci. After arriving unannounced at Uptown with twenty-nine songs on three cassette tapes, the North Carolina natives had instantly mesmerized Heavy D and Harrell with their smooth sound. "We didn't have an appointment," group member Devante later said. "I didn't even know who Andre Harrell was, but I knew what Uptown was, and I wanted us to be there."

Four-member boy bands, such as Boyz II Men and Color Me Badd, were already dominating the charts. Combs knew he had to make Jodeci stand out from the crowd. He turned to his then-girlfriend Misa

Hylton, who was interning at Def Jam in artist development, to help create a unique look for the group. Hylton and Combs had both grown up in Mount Vernon, where he lived around the corner from her best friend, Tiffany. The two had started their relationship after reuniting at the Apollo Theater in Harlem. Hylton helped Combs fashion an urban, hard-edged look for Jodeci, dressing them in baseball hats and jerseys, baggy jeans, army fatigues, leather outfits, jewelry, and sunglasses.

At the time, Combs was still throwing "Daddy's House" parties around New York City. Cooper dubbed these gatherings "the first to mesh the uptown black and Latino crowd with the preppy white college kids of New York University and Columbia."[2]

Combs used the parties as somewhat of a focus group, getting inspiration from the bold street styles worn by partygoers. "[Jodeci was] like a piece of clay I thought I could mold into something, so I decided to take the way I was seeing kids dressing in the streets," Combs has said.[3]

In trying to market Jodeci, Combs came up with an original approach that is now widely used across the music industry. He put together a "street team" of twenty teenagers, who passed out promotional stickers and postcards in housing projects. The team also went to nightclubs to convince deejays to play new songs by Uptown artists. They would then hit the dance floor to generate buzz. The efforts were successful—all of Jodeci's first three singles hit #1 on the Billboard R&B/Hip-Hop charts and the album *Forever My Lady* went triple platinum.

Around this time, Combs also started playing with a new idea: "Remixing" Jodeci's slow ballads together with popular hip-hop beats. With the title of a later album, Combs claimed he "invented" the remix, a statement that some music magazines hotly debated. He married the group's No. 1 hit "Come and Talk to Me" with rap group EPMD's "You're a Customer." The remix moved the group toward the more urban sound it adopted on later songs and albums.

Combs's career was finally taking flight. But not everything he touched turned to platinum. In 1991, he decided to capitalize on the fame he'd earned through hosting "Daddy's House" parties and his connections in the music business by putting together a benefit basketball game. His aim was to raise funds for AIDS awareness and research in the wake of NBA player Magic Johnson's diagnosis. Johnson, a world-famous basketball player on the Los Angeles Lakers, had shocked the world that November with his announcement that he was HIV-positive.

Heavy D agreed to cohost the event, and the "First Annual Celebrity Holiday Basketball Classic" was born. Combs's team, "The Puff Daddy All-Stars" (comprised of Combs, Jodeci, Father MC, and other rising stars), would take on the "Heavsters," aka Heavy D and his "boyz," on the court.

Combs convinced City College of New York to host the event in their gym. In return, he agreed to pay $1,850 to the school, guarantee attendance of at least twenty celebrities, and cover the cost of liability insurance. He then set about promoting the event, working with local radio station KISS-FM to generate interest. Security officers and police were enlisted to help control the expected crowds.

On game day (December 28, 1991), thousands of people showed up to snag a seat in the 2,730-seat gym. When it became clear not everyone would fit inside, the crowd became restless and broke through the doors. It was impossible to control the throngs of angry people trying to get inside. Ultimately, twenty-nine people were injured and nine killed in the stampede. Among the victims who died was a close friend of Combs's girlfriend Hylton.

Days later, when Combs resurfaced in public at the Plaza Hotel, he talked about how devastated he was that the event had gone horribly wrong. "In addition to sponsoring a profitable event, my dream for this evening was to bring a positive program to my people, to people of my age and to people of my community," Combs told the *New York Times* in 1992.

Public scrutiny followed. Had Combs oversold the event, bringing about the disastrous results? Why hadn't he gotten liability insurance? The tragedy affected Combs both personally and professionally. The *New York Post* ran a cover story titled "The Fool Named Puff Daddy." Harrell asked Combs not to report to work for a while, although he did secure lawyers for Combs. According to *Vibe* reporter Dream Hampton, Combs even received death threats and considered suicide at one point.

"After the incident, it was like I was crazy, losing my mind . . . thinking about the people who died, thinking about the families, thinking about their pain," Combs said. "For a while, I was probably clinically insane." The nightmare would follow Combs for years to come. He faced almost a dozen wrongful death and personal injury lawsuits, the last of which he settled in 2000 with a survivor named Nicole Levy.

But as the cliché decrees, "the show must go on." Combs soon snapped back into 24/7 work mode to bring his Uptown artists to fame. One of his protégés was young Mary J. Blige, a seventeen-year-old R&B singer. Uptown had signed Blige after her father sent Harrell a mall karaoke recording of Blige singing

Anita Baker's "Caught Up in the Rapture." Combs got "goose bumps" the first time he heard her voice. He immediately saw the star power inherent in the street-savvy singer: "In Mary, I saw an inner pain, an inner beauty, an inner artistry," Combs told *i-D* magazine's Frank Broughton.

He worked closely with Blige to executive produce her debut album, *What's the 411?* The debut was highly praised, earning Blige comparisons to famous R&B divas, such as Baker and Chaka Khan. It also had crossover power, charting not only at No. 1 on the R&B charts but hitting No. 6 on the Billboard 200 chart, which covers all genres. It became clear that Combs's magic touch played a big part in many Uptown artists' success. "I was a wonder kid," Combs told Oprah in 2006.

Combs's magic touch did not go unnoticed at Uptown, but neither did his overconfident attitude. Coworkers recall Combs standing in the hallway shirtless, saying "Puff Daddy is my name as an artist, Sean Combs is my name for the movies." When colleagues would try to give him direction, Combs refused to listen, saying, "I don't work for you, I work for Dre" (referring to Harrell). The office tension coupled with the fallout from the basketball incident put a strain on Harrell's and Combs's relationship. In mid-1993, Combs was fired.

At the time, Combs was stunned. He ended up sitting on the stoop of Harrell's home later that evening "crying his eyes out." In the space of five short years, he'd rocketed through the ranks from intern to a vice president role. Where had he gone wrong? Combs called it "one of the worst days of [my] life;" he felt "heartbroken" that he'd disappointed his mentor Harrell.

Yet with time, Combs would later gain a different perspective on what had happened. "Getting fired was one of the best things that could have happened to me," Combs said in an interview with Oprah Winfrey in 2006. "It taught me that putting out a record is a team effort. It taught me how to motivate people. It taught me not to get caught up in my own hype. I'm glad I learned that at a young age."

Never one to wallow, Combs had to come up with Plan B—quickly. While at Uptown, Combs had been developing his own upstart company, Bad Boy Entertainment, with Harrell's encouragement. The company would be not only a record label, but also a management firm and production company. He had gone as far as creating a logo (a likeness of his toddler godson wearing giant combat boots) and starting to nurture new artists under the Bad Boy umbrella. Now it was time for Combs to bring the dream to life and show the world what he had to offer—on his terms.

"My only regret is that if I had any flaws, I could have been nurtured or corrected instead of people giving up on me," Combs told *Vibe* three days after being fired. "But I'm not ungrateful for what I've received. This is just another chapter. This ain't no sad ending."

Chapter 4

THINKING B.I.G.

L egend has it that when Harrell fired Combs, he told him, "There can only be one lion in the jungle."[1] Combs agreed, later telling Oprah, "There can't be two kings in one castle."

Though Combs was more than ready to be the king of his own domain, he still needed to find a home within the music industry. At the time, he was temporarily running Bad Boy Entertainment on a small budget out of his mother's house in Westchester, New York.

Surprisingly, Combs was still in close contact with Harrell, who helped him review the contracts and offers that were coming his way. Harrell suggested he court Arista Records founder and mogul Clive Davis, who had helped artists, such as Whitney Houston, shoot to superstardom. "After what I've done for you, Clive Davis, the songman, can only take you to another good place," Harrell told Combs.[2]

The idea came to fruition. In 1994, Clive Davis bought a 50 percent stake in Bad Boy Entertainment. Combs's ambition impressed him. Davis felt that joining forces with Bad Boy would help Arista establish a foothold in the hip-hop genre. He later said that Combs wowed him by being "unusual in his marketing perspective, creative visions, sense of himself and the music he wanted to do."[3] The admiration was mutual. Combs said that Davis's focus on the music, rather than the money, won him over.

Following the deal, Combs wasted no time setting up a stylish office at the corner of 19th Street and Fifth Avenue. The office's walls displayed signs, such as "Losing Is For Losers" and "Sleeping Is Forbidden." His office resembled that of a mogul, with a giant desk, huge sound system, and a tropical fish tank built into the wall separating him from his employees. A large picture of Motown founder Berry Gordy set the tone for what Combs planned to accomplish.

"I definitely took a page out of the Motown book when I was starting my company, as far as having a young cultural lifestyle movement through my music. [I wanted] to really sell black music in a positive way, an urgent way," Combs said on *NY1.com* in 2003.

To that end, Combs put together a "dream team" featuring general manager Kirk Burrows, his old Howard University friend Deric Angelettie, and fellow Howard alums Harve Pierre, Chucky Thompson, and Nashiem Myrick. He felt it was important to surround himself with people who knew his past and believed in his future.

In those early days of Bad Boy Entertainment, Combs's efforts revolved mainly around two artists. He worked closely with rappers Craig Mack and Christopher "Biggie Smalls" Wallace, also known as the Notorious B.I.G. Both came from rough backgrounds: Mack hailed from Long Island, where he was rumored to be homeless, and Wallace had been a drug dealer in Brooklyn. As the first releases of Bad Boy, their albums dropped within one week of each other in September 1994.

To promote the two artists, Combs designed an innovative "B.I.G. Mack Sampler" press kit and cassette sampler. The package featured a cassette tape with six songs from each rapper and a glossy flyer designed to look like fast-food marketing that read "Serving Up the Two Hottest Platters on the Street." Mack's single "Flava in Ya Ear" was an immediate hit, reaching No. 9 on the Billboard Hot 100 and No. 4 on the R&B/Hip-Hop Songs chart.

Though Mack was the first to resonate with audiences on a large scale, it was Wallace who ultimately changed the hip-hop landscape. Combs had first discovered the towering rapper, who was 6 feet 3 and weighed in at more than 300 pounds, while Combs was still working at Uptown. *The Source* writer Matty C passed him a demo tape from the unsigned young rapper. Instantly magnetized by Wallace's catchy style and ultracool persona, Combs saw the potential in working with him.

"When I met him, I had this dream of a company, and all he wanted to do was be a rapper," remembered Combs. "I thanked God, not because he sent me a dope rapper, but because he sent me somebody who cared for me. I needed that."

Though Wallace's explicit lyrics hadn't been the right fit at Uptown, the approach fit well with the raw vibe Combs was trying to create at Bad Boy. In preparing *Ready to Die,* Wallace's first album, Combs fought to include radio-friendly, catchier songs like "Juicy," "One More Chance," and "Big Poppa," alongside the grittier "gangsta" fare Wallace preferred. *Rolling Stone* later asserted that the album was a game changer that "map[ped] out the sound of Nineties cool," naming it the eighth best album of the 1990s and one of its 500 Greatest Albums of All-Time. "When he was on that mic, it was like listening to a miracle," Combs told *Vibe* in 2006.

Combs rode the wave of his company's mounting success. He often made cameo appearances in his artists' music videos and lent vocal tracks to kick off the songs. This type of exposure meshed with his behind-the-scenes credibility made Combs a contender for the same type of success enjoyed by those for whom he produced and wrote songs. "Codirecting and costarring in the videos of Mary J. Blige and Jodeci—the jewels in his young crown of achievement—he inspired the same kind of awe and jealousy usually reserved for a front-and-center star," wrote Scott Poulson-Bryant in *Vibe* in 1993. "Puffy has the aura of a performer; quite possibly he is the only A&R executive in the business with as many groupies as his artists."

Along with making his *own* mark on Bad Boy songs, he also created a great deal of synergy between Bad Boy artists. For instance, Wallace rapped the intro to the remix of Mack's "Flava in Ya Ear," while Mary J. Blige, Total, and Faith Evans lent their voices to Wallace's song, "One More Chance." The video for the same song featured cameos by a slew of music stars, including Heavy D, Queen Latifah, TLC's "T-Boz," Aaliyah, and many more. Combs was also shown palling around with Wallace and hanging out in a hot tub with beautiful women, including Misa Hylton-Brim.

The friendship between Combs and Wallace wasn't just on screen. Outside of their business relationship, the two developed a friendship, often laughing, joking, and meeting up at places such as Junior's restaurant in Brooklyn. Combs also kept Wallace focused. He didn't want him to fall back into bad habits like drug dealing. "Before [Biggie] signed his deal, he was worried about getting in trouble with the law," Combs's former assistant Sybil Pennix told *Vibe* in 2012, adding that she hid Wallace's gun in her desk so he wouldn't have access to it. Combs was the right person to get him on track: "Puffy went the extra mile. . . . I told Big I would rather he be with somebody [like Puffy] that was young, black, business-savvy, and hungry," DJ Mister Cee shared in the same *Vibe* article.

During this time, Wallace had also struck up a friendship with fellow rapper Tupac Shakur, who was affiliated with Death Row Records. This West Coast-based music label played home to artists such as Dr. Dre and Snoop Dogg.

Wallace and Shakur had first met in 1992 on the set of the movie *Poetic Justice*. The two had become fast friends. Since their first meeting, the two had recorded a few duets, one of which later appeared on Wallace's posthumous *The Biggie Duets* album. They even freestyled onstage together at Madison Square Garden for the Budweiser Superfest.

Yet their friendship was a rocky one. Shakur publicly accused Wallace of lifting lyrics from his albums. He soon accused him of much more than that. In 1994, Shakur received an offer from Jimmy "Henchman" Rosemond to lay down vocals on a track for Little Shawn at New York's Quad Recording Studios. Shakur agreed, but only if he could be paid the fee of $7,000 the same evening. Rosemond promised that Andre Harrell would be present at the studio to give Shakur the money.

When Shakur arrived at the studio that evening, he was ambushed in the lobby by two men wearing army fatigues. The men stole Shakur's money and jewelry and then shot Shakur multiple times. After the shooting, a stunned Shakur and his crew rode the elevator to the eighth floor, where Little Shawn was recording in the studio accompanied by Combs, Harrell, Wallace, and at least thirty others. Disoriented and badly injured, Shakur became convinced that all of them were involved with setting him up. He later shared these accusations with *Vibe* magazine.

The incident drove a wedge even further between the East Coast and West Coast rap groups. East Coast artists had dominated the rap scene throughout the '70s and '80s. But the West Coast started coming to prominence in the late '80s and early '90s with its more dance-friendly vibe. Tension had been building between the two coasts since the early '90s, when East Coast rapper Tim Dog released a song dissing West Coast trio N.W.A. The faces of the feud ultimately became Bad Boy and Death Row records.

As the East Coast and West Coast rivalry started to heat up, Combs did his best to put a lid on the allegations. Combs also wrote Shakur a letter to let him know that he and Wallace had no prior knowledge or involvement about what had happened at Quad Recording Studios. Reportedly, Shakur answered by saying, "Well, Puff, everything's cool. It ain't no problem like that."[4]

At the end of 1995, Combs arranged a meeting in Los Angeles with Rosemond, Shakur, J. Prince, and Death Row Records mogul Suge Knight. He wanted them to resolve the issue. He also wanted to offer to collaborate with Shakur and Death Row Records. But when Shakur entered the room, he angrily pointed at Rosemond, saying "Them . . . shot me."

Though the meeting did nothing to improve rap relations across coasts, Combs's Bad Boy label was reaching a fever pitch of success. Blige and Wallace were firmly established as superstars, while other Bad Boy artists were also rising through the ranks. Female trio Total, who had started out providing background vocals for Wallace, had a big hit with "Can't You See." The song appeared on the *New Jersey Drive* soundtrack and featured a rap intro from Wallace. Their self-titled album went platinum, as did that of Bad Boy R&B artist Faith Evans, who married Wallace in 1994.

The industry took notice of Combs's talents. In 1996, the American Society of Composers, Authors and Publishers (ASCAP) awarded him with "Songwriter of the Year" honors. Though Combs was certainly deserving of the honor, he later admitted that he doesn't consider songwriting one of his strengths. "I'm not the greatest songwriter, but I can say I've worked with some of the greatest," he said on *Inside the Actor's Studio*. "My strength is as a producer; my strength was never sitting there freestyling, writing. I was always one of the best when it came time to put on the live show—the way the lights should look, the way we should present ourselves. I was always great at playing my position."

Not everyone was as complimentary of Combs's accomplishments, however. Suge Knight fueled the hostile fire between Death Row and Bad Boy at the Source Awards in August 1995 with an obvious insult. "If you don't want the owner of your label on your album or in your video or on your tour, come sign with Death Row," he taunted. Combs was shocked at Knight's audacity. During his turn at the podium that night, he made a plea for East Coast–West Coast unity, even giving Death Row artist Snoop Dogg a hug. "I couldn't believe what [Knight] said," Combs told *Vibe* in 1995. "I thought we was boys."

One month later, another incident sealed the bad blood between the two coasts. Combs, Wallace, and Wallace's protégés Junior M.A.F.I.A. attended a birthday party for music producer Jermaine Dupri at Atlanta's Platinum House nightclub. That evening, Suge Knight's friend Jake Robles was shot and killed. Knight accused Combs of being involved with the shooting. "Right then, [Knight] was like, 'I think you had something to do with this,'" Combs told *Vibe* in the same interview. "I'm like, 'What are you talking about? I was standing right here with you!' I felt really sorry for him . . . he was showing me his insecurity."

The feud played out in media headlines and on radio stations and TV screens across America. Shakur insisted Wallace's song "Who Shot Ya" was about the incident at Quad Recording Studios. Wallace claimed he wrote the song long before. Shakur retaliated with

"Hit 'Em Up," on which he claimed that Evans had cheated on Wallace with him. Death Row artists Tha Dogg Pound made a video titled "New York, New York." The video featured giants stomping on Manhattan. During the video shoot in Brooklyn, someone shot at one of the set trailers. East Coast artists Tragedy, Capone, Noreaga, and Mobb Deep later responded with a video for "LA, LA," in which people resembling members of Tha Dogg Pound were kidnapped and thrown off a New York bridge.

Combs did his best to maintain business as usual. However, he did beef up personal security. Back at Bad Boy, he signed new artists 112 (a four-member male quartet) and Mase. Following the formula that had brought his other artists fame, he enlisted Mase to rap on 112's first hit single "Only You" and a single from Wallace's upcoming album *Life After Death* titled "Mo Money, Mo Problems." Combs also began planting the seeds for a career crossover. He was preparing songs for his own rap debut album.

In March 1996, the East Coast–West Coast rivalry came to a chilling head. At the Soul Train Awards in Los Angeles, Wallace and Shakur saw each other for the first time in person since the Quad Recording Studios shooting. Wallace later told *Vibe* that it was "the first time I really looked into [Shakur's] face." Wallace said that he was unsettled by the wild look in

Shakur's eyes. Afterward, their entourages faced off in the parking lot, with both sides pulling weapons. Though no one was harmed, that wouldn't be the case for much longer.

Six months later, on September 7, 1996, Shakur was shot four times in Las Vegas after a boxing match. He was rushed to the Southern Nevada University Medical Center. He died six days later. The rap world reeled from the devastating loss, and the rivalry felt all too real. When journalist Dream Hampton called Wallace the next day to get his reaction, all he could say was, "Shocked."

What had started as a war of words had ended in the tragic killing of a talented, young rap legend in the making. "The tragedy of Tupac is that his untimely passing is representative of too many black men in this country," wrote Quincy Jones in the foreword for *Tupac Shakur.* "If we had lost Oprah Winfrey at 25, we would have lost a relatively unknown, local market TV anchorwoman. If we had lost Malcolm X at 25, we would have lost a hustler named Detroit Red. And if I had left the world at 25, we would have lost a big-band trumpet player and aspiring composer—just a sliver of my eventual life potential."

Sadly, Christopher Wallace never got the chance to reach his full potential either. At the Soul Train Awards in March 1997 in Los Angeles, Wallace,

Combs, and 112 took the stage to present the award for "Best R&B Soul Single Female." When Wallace read Toni Braxton's name as the winner, the audience loudly booed him. Wallace took it in stride, joking, "What's up, Cali?" He was in good spirits, as his new album *Life After Death* was about to be released. Wallace believed it might help clear up the tension between the coasts.

"He felt that when the album came out, it was going to clear up a lot of stuff, because over the past few years, there had been so-called controversy," Combs told a reporter. "He wanted to represent on his album not feeding into the negativity; he felt proud that he didn't do that. [Wallace] was just trying to make good music and represent for everyone internationally as a whole."

The next day, the Bad Boy entourage attended a *Vibe* magazine after-party at Petersen Automotive Museum. After the party was shut down due to overcrowding around 12:30 A.M., they exited the party in two Chevy Suburbans. Combs was in one of the cars with three bodyguards. Wallace was in the second car with three others. At a nearby stoplight, a Chevrolet Impala pulled up next to Wallace's vehicle. Its driver shot twenty-four-year-old Wallace several times in the chest. He died before they could make it to a nearby hospital.

The somber funeral back in Brooklyn was like a "Who's Who" of hip-hop. Wife Faith Evans sang "Walk With Me, Lord" and Combs performed the eulogy. Also present were Mary J. Blige, Flava Flav, Queen Latifah, Lil' Kim, Busta Rhymes, and many others who cared about and worked with Wallace. Crying fans lined the streets of Brooklyn as the hearse drove by. They chanted the name "Biggie" as his music played on full blast.

The timeline of events that followed was eerie. Three weeks later, Wallace's double-disc album *Life After Death* was released. The album featured irresistible dance hits such as "Hypnotize" and "Mo Money, Mo Problems," which included a rap verse from Combs. Aggressive songs such as "Kick in the Door" and "Somebody's Got to Die" were also part of the lineup. Though the versatile approach was a bit of a gamble, it worked. "Rarely has a rapper attempted to please so many different audiences—and done it so brilliantly," raved the *Los Angeles Times.*

It was also hard to ignore the foreboding elements of the release. Along with the title, the album cover featured the larger-than-life rapper standing against a hearse. Numerous songs referenced dying young or receiving death threats. Yet insiders insisted that the content was meant to symbolize what Wallace viewed as a new beginning. One song, "Going Back to Cali," was even meant to be a tribute to his West Coast counterparts.

Combs had toyed with shelving the release after the murder, but Wallace's family provided the motivation to forge ahead. "When it happened, I was like 'We're not putting out the album,'" Combs recalled to *The Fader* in 2011. "His family and friends were like, 'Are you bugging? We've gotta put it out now.' But with [the music], his legacy lives, he doesn't become someone that was here for one album and disappeared. . . . That was the closest thing to having him here—hearing his music."

It became obvious that Wallace's fans agreed, as the end product was a smash success. Entering the charts at No. 1, the album was eventually certified "Diamond" (more than 10 million copies sold) by the Recording Industry Association of America (RIAA). "[Wallace's] impact on the world can be seen every time a Biggie song gets played on the radio, at the club, at a stadium or in a car driving down the street," said Rob Stone, a one-time Arista executive who has worked with both Combs and Wallace. "I hope we can all learn a lot from him, his music and his legacy. I'm always amazed by the particular new details and nuances I pick up each time I listen to his music. He was truly the best that ever did it."

No doubt about it, both Shakur and Notorious B.I.G. left a lasting imprint on the hip-hop world. Today, almost two decades later, both artists are still considered pioneers in the rap field. However, their legacy is clouded by mystery and tragedy. Theories abound about who committed the murders and why, with both Combs and Knight implicated at times. The Los Angeles Police Department was also accused of covering up information. Voletta Wallace, Biggie's mom, sued the LAPD for mishandling the case in 2002. To date, both murders have gone unsolved, though Jimmy Rosemond did confess in 2012 that he was involved in Shakur's Quad Studios shooting.

In the aftermath, Combs was shell-shocked by the sudden loss, left to do the only thing he knew how—move forward. Though Notorious B.I.G. was gone, Combs was about to make sure he would never be forgotten.

Chapter 5

SUDDENLY IN THE SPOTLIGHT

T hroughout the 1990s, Combs had focused his energy on conquering the music industry from behind the scenes. Now he longed to step into the limelight. While his close friend and collaborator Christopher "Notorious B.I.G." Wallace was still alive, Combs had enlisted Wallace to help coach his fledgling rap career and teach him the tricks of the performing trade.

"Puff sat me down and said 'Yo, I want you to manage me,' [but] before I said yes, I had to ask him why," Wallace was quoted as saying. "He was like,

'Who could teach me how to be the best artist but the best artist?'"[1]

Now Combs was ready to pay tribute to Wallace and show off all he had learned from his late mentor. He enlisted Wallace's widow, Faith Evans, and Bad Boy artists 112 to come together to record a tribute song titled "I'll Be Missing You." Set to a sample of the Police's 1984 hit "I'll Be Watching You," the song provided a moving love letter from the Bad Boy "family" to the friend they missed so much. Released two months after Wallace's death, it was an immediate smash hit. The song became only the fifth in history to enter the Billboard chart at No. 1, staying there for eleven weeks.

Combs capitalized on the success, continuing to prepare his first solo album for debut later that year. Some of the songs were altered to reflect his feelings about Wallace's death. One in particular, titled "Pain," addressed the deaths of Combs's father and Wallace, as well as the City College basketball disaster. The title of the album was also changed from *Hell Up in Harlem* to *No Way Out*.

No Way Out was released in July 1997. The album was significant not only in that it was Combs's debut as a rapper, but it also marked a dramatic shift in hip-hop music in general. After the deaths of Tupac and Biggie, fans started to move toward lighter, more upbeat fare rather than hard-core, "gangster"-style rap. Artists such as Will Smith and Combs (aka "Puff Daddy") personified the new hip-hop royalty. Mainstream radio listeners and MTV addicts embraced their flashy, fun vibe. The album was a huge success, with such hits as "Can't Nobody Hold Me Down" and "It's All About the Benjamins." It sold more than 7 million copies. It also won a slew of American Music Awards, Soul Train Awards, and even a Grammy.

Later that year, Combs put together a massive tour to promote *No Way Out*, kicking it off in November 1997 in Detroit. Though he acted as the headliner, the concert also featured an array of heavy-hitter acts, including Usher, Lil' Kim, Busta Rhymes, Jay-Z, Foxy Brown, and his Bad Boy protégé Mase. As the *Baltimore Sun* put it, "If all you went by was chart clout, Puff Daddy & The Family's 'No Way Out' World Tour would be the road show of the decade." Combs was thrilled with the lineup, telling MTV, "I'm a fan of all these people helping to support me."

True to form, the tour also gave Combs a platform for cross-promoting Bad Boy artists. At one point during the stage show, Combs and Mase stormed the stage together in shiny suits to sing "Been Around the World" and Mase's hit, "Feel So Good." At another, Notorious B.I.G. videos graced the giant video screens.

At the end of the show, all of the artists took the stage in Bad Boy jerseys to dance to Sister Sledge's song, "We Are Family," as balloons dropped from above.

The show was also a chance for Combs to explore the nuances of his dual stage personality. "When the spotlight finally hits me on stage, I'm going to be cool. I'm going to turn into Puff Daddy," he told MTV during a behind-the-scenes documentary. "When I'm nervous before I make my entrance, I'm going to be Sean Combs, but when I finally hit it, I'm going to be Puff Daddy." It turned out there was no need for Combs to be nervous—the tour ultimately broke records and grossed $15 million.

In its own way, the tour also signified the way hip-hop was evolving. Combs later called it a "changing point in hip-hop history." Most promoters had stopped investing in hip-hop tours due to fears of violence. The *No Way Out* tour symbolized a renewal of faith. "There were no big tours concerning rap because there was so much negativity," Mase said at the time. "We're trying to change that, to have a successful tour with nobody being locked up or nobody being harmed. We'll open doors for other rap groups to go out and have a good time without everybody being so scared."

For Combs, it was the realization of a dream he had begun cultivating as a young boy in Harlem.

While growing up, he'd attended a high-energy Run DMC rap concert at Madison Square Garden and told himself that one day he'd perform on its legendary stage. "The first night I played the Garden, I could hear people chanting my name," Combs told Oprah in 2006. "As I looked out over the crowd, I was bugging out. It was incredible and definitely a blessing."

Another highlight of the album was Combs's megaperformance of "I'll Be Missing You" at the 1997 MTV Video Music Awards. Accompanied by a full choir, Faith Evans, 112, and former "Police" member Sting, whose original song had been sampled, Combs provided a memorable rendition of his hit song. The performance was dedicated not only to Notorious B.I.G., but also other notable late greats, such as Princess Diana. The beloved British royal had died the same year in a tragic car crash. Later that night, Combs accepted awards on behalf of the late Notorious B.I.G. accompanied by Wallace's mother, Voletta, and Faith Evans.

The Grammy Awards were another major milestone, with Combs collecting the first of several in his career for "Best Rap Album." Not everyone was as thrilled about the win as Combs, though. When *No Way Out* beat Wu-Tang Clan's *Wu-Tang Forever,* rapper ODB stormed the stage and stole the microphone, saying, "I went out and bought me an outfit that costed me a lot of money today. . . . Puffy is good, but Wu-Tang is the best."

It wasn't the first time that Combs would encounter criticism of or resistance toward his quick ascent to success. But he refused to let it hold him back. Reflecting on it in 1997, Combs said, "It was the biggest year for me as a recording artist. I was kinda big already in the music industry, but this was the year for me as a recording artist [in which] I got all the respectful accolades . . . and the biggest-selling hip-hop tour in history. It was one of those huge crossover times for hip-hop because all my videos were in heavy rotation."

For Combs, being so busy was a welcome distraction from the grief that plagued him since losing Wallace. "You couldn't have told me I was gong to make it out of that, emotionally and spiritually," Combs told *The Fader* in 2011. "[I thought] my life was over after that."

Combs kept moving forward, masterminding his own high-profile crossover projects. For the remix of a *No Way Out* song called "It's All About the Benjamins," he enlisted rocker Dave Grohl (of Nirvana and Foo Fighters) to add heavy guitar and vocals. He started working with pop diva Mariah Carey, producing several of her tracks and rapping on the songs "Fantasy" and "Honey," alongside Bad Boy artists the Lox and Mase. Combs also lent his talents to fast-rising star Jennifer Lopez for her debut album *On the Six.* One report said that for the year of 1997, Combs had involvement as either producer or artist in an unprecedented 40 percent of that year's No. 1 Billboard hits.

"The thing I can appreciate about Puff is that . . . you can go into any club and from 12:30 on, every hit they're playing, it's a Bad Boy hit," actor and friend Malcolm-Jamal Warner said in 2009.

The wave of success ushered in somewhat of a role reversal for Combs and his former mentor, Andre Harrell. In 1998, Combs hired Harrell as a consultant and to take over chief executive duties at Bad Boy Entertainment. Harrell had been fired from a high-profile position running Motown Records and was ready to reunite with his one-time protégé.

Around this time, Combs also began working with a young artist named Jamal "Shyne" Barrow. Shyne's rap style bore a striking resemblance to Notorious B.I.G. He had been discovered after a talent scout heard him rapping in a barbershop and made an introduction to Combs. It was reported that Combs signed him for one million dollars, though the actual amount was never verified. Combs immediately took the young rapper under his wing, showing him the ropes of the music industry.

"That was when he was like the Michael Jackson of hip-hop," Shyne told the *Village Voice*. "I went everywhere with him. That was the relationship. I was just watching Michael Jackson at work. Combs was one of the biggest people in the world, and I was just going along for the joyride."

The "joyride" was moving full speed ahead, as Combs was busy prepping his second album, *Forever*. Shyne would appear on the album aside a powerful list of celebrity collaborators, including Lil' Kim, R. Kelly, Bizzy Bone (of Bone Thugs-n-Harmony), Busta Rhymes, and Cee-Lo Green among others. In December 1998, Combs flew an equally impressive group of trusted producers and collaborators down to the Bahamas for recording sessions.

Yet if 1997 was a charmed year for Combs, 1999 was the opposite. Though it debuted at No. 2 on the Billboard charts, *Forever* was released to mixed reviews. It did not have any memorable hits. *People* magazine wrote: "Combs should stick to what he does best: making hits for other people."

Bad Boy was flailing as well. Mase decided to leave the label and retire for religious reasons. Rap trio the Lox defected to Ruff Ryder Entertainment. Faith Evans had publicly accused Combs in *Elle* magazine of not sharing any of the royalties from their hit "I'll Be Missing You." She also said that she hadn't seen "a dime" of the money from her solo album, which had been released years earlier. The label responded that the money from "I'll Be Missing You" had gone to charity and into a trust fund for Wallace's children and that all royalties with her solo album were being resolved. Yet the damage was done. The *Washington Post* ran an article titled "The Deflation of Puffy Combs," alleging that Combs's career was on the decline.

That year, Combs had also begun dating actress and singer Jennifer Lopez, whom he had met on the set of his video "Been Around the World." The relationship was somewhat controversial. Combs had just had a baby in April 1998 with girlfriend Kim Porter and had been living with her before abruptly moving on to Lopez. Many people felt they flaunted their high-profile relationship, making a spectacle of themselves on red carpets and in the media. "Her misadventures with boyfriend Sean 'Puffy' Combs have been watched as closely as those of Liz Taylor and Richard Burton in another era," wrote *Vanity Fair* in 2000.

The controversy did not stop. On December 27, 1999, Lopez and Combs spent an evening at Club New York with a group of friends. While leaving the nightclub around 2:55 A.M., their entourage got into a verbal scuffle with another group and gunshots were fired. No one was killed, but three people were injured in the crossfire. Two of the shooting victims claimed that they'd seen Combs with a gun. Nine witnesses said that Jamal "Shyne" Barrow had also been carrying a gun.

Accompanied by Combs's bodyguard and driver, Combs and Lopez fled the scene in a Lincoln Navigator, running eleven red lights before they were pulled over by police. Police then found a gun in the vehicle, though they determined it was not the same gun used in the shooting. Since no one would claim the gun, all four were arrested on gun possession charges and brought into the police station. Lopez was later released and cleared of all charges.

"I was scared to death. I didn't commit the crime," Combs later told Oprah. "There are so many things I want to do, and sitting in jail isn't one of them. But I knew the reality of how many people of color are convicted of crimes they didn't commit."

To clear his name, Combs hired high-profile lawyers Benjamin Brafman and Johnnie L. Cochran, Jr., who had previously represented O. J. Simpson in his infamous murder trial. The eventual trial that ensued was a media circus. Fans stood outside the courthouse with signs reading "Hip Hop Needs You" and "Keep Puffy Free." Cochran called it "the biggest celebrity trial in the country since the Simpson case."

Combs was ultimately acquitted of all five counts against him. The verdict was a tremendous relief to Combs, who *MTV.com* reported "rocked back and forth with emotion, shook his head in relief and finally gave a wide, relaxed grin." However, Jamal "Shyne" Barrow didn't fare so well. He was convicted on two counts of assault, two weapons charges, and reckless endangerment—and sentenced to ten years in prison. Combs called Barrow's sentence "unfair and extreme," saying, "I'm shocked by today's outcome. I will continue to support Shyne throughout his appeal."

Combs and Lopez tried to pick up the pieces and move on with life as usual. In February 2000, the two once again made headlines as they attended the Grammy Awards. But they couldn't escape the nightclub debacle. Grammy host Rosie O'Donnell made pointed barbs about the shooting, prompting Combs to leave before the awards show concluded. The pressure of the trial and the media attention proved too much for the high-profile relationship. They broke up in early 2001.

"We'll always be friends," Combs told *Jet*. "I'll always love her, you know. I just want her to be happy. It's been a rough year. We went through a lot of things, and I'm just glad the whole ordeal is over."

With things at Bad Boy Entertainment rocky and the trial taking a stressful toll, Combs felt like he had lost his mogul mojo. He'd planned on releasing an all-star gospel album titled *Thank You* with artists such as Brandy, 112, Brian McKnight, and Faith Evans (who was still under contract despite the problems between her and Combs). However, the project was shelved. It was time for Combs to regroup and step out of the spotlight.

"It's like a mini-retirement," he stated. "I feel like everybody is asking, 'So, what now?' And I have always had the answer . . . but I really want to handle this differently. I want to make sure that I am not in this situation ever again. So I need time to make sure that I just look at my life as a whole, from the beginning of my life to now. . . . I really want to take time for myself as a person."

Though he was down, Combs certainly wasn't out. The father of reinvention was about to make his mark in a whole new way.

Chapter 6

MORE THAN MUSIC

Acommon lyric heard in many of Sean Combs's songs is "We won't stop." For Combs, that motto has held especially true in his professional career. Combs's dream doesn't stop with music. For Combs, being an entrepreneur means creating a complete lifestyle brand from top to bottom.

"My dream was that you would wake up in the morning, your alarm would go off, one of my records would be playing. You'd get in the shower and use my shampoo, then you would get out and use the beauty products. You'd get dressed and put on Sean John [clothing], and then you would go to work," Combs has said of his overall vision. "After work, you would go and change into your evening wear . . . and you'd put on Sean John again, spray on another of my fragrances, stop by and have a drink of Ciroc [Combs's drink brand]. And then maybe take your young lady out to a movie that I was starring in."

For many of his fans, that vision isn't far from reality. Over the last two decades, Combs has not only built an empire with Bad Boy Entertainment, but also ventured into acting, magazine publishing, restaurant ownership, fashion, brand endorsements, event planning, and much more. "I'm in such a unique lane. To be honest, it's not a lane a lot of hip-hop artists want to be in. My lane is entertainment. My lane is celebration," Combs has said.

Once Combs did start branching out from Bad Boy, it's not surprising that he entered the fashion arena first. After all, the stage was set for Combs to make a splash on the style scene from an early age. At six years old, Combs's mother, Janice, put on a fashion show at a local day-care center, and young Combs hit the catwalk. "I came out and tried to steal the show," Combs said. "As soon as that spotlight hit me, I just embraced it."[1]

As an adult, Combs has commanded the catwalk in an entirely different fashion—as the mastermind behind Sean John Clothing. Since the apparel company's founding in 1998, Sean John has grown by leaps and bounds with retail sales of more than $525 million annually.

Combs first debuted the men's streetwear line in spring 1999. His aim was to fill what he viewed as a "big void in the market for an upscale 'urban high-fashion line.'" To gain credibility and insider knowledge of the fashion industry, Combs joined forces with Jeffrey Tweedy, a former executive for fashion lines Ralph Lauren and Karl Kani. Urban audiences quickly flocked to Sean John's fashion-forward denim flight suits, velour sweat suits, and 3-D tees. Stores, such as Bloomingdale's, couldn't keep stock on the shelves. Sales also went through the roof after Combs wore a Sean John hat on "Saturday Night Live." The venture was deemed an instant success.

"Other designers . . . have borrowed styles from the streets without much success. Sean John kept it real, blending Puffy's taste for ghetto-fabulous gear with thugged-out B-boy flavor," wrote *Vibe* magazine.

That year, Combs sought to achieve legitimacy by throwing a giant "coming-out" party for his new clothing line in Paris, widely considered the capital of high fashion. Designers from Chanel, Christian Dior, and Jean Paul Gaultier mingled with models such as Kate Moss and moguls such as Andre Harrell. In fall

2000, the collection debuted at prestigious Fashion Week in New York with a show attended by such celebrities as Tommy Hilfiger, Missy Elliott, and Derek Jeter. *Vibe* dubbed the show "one of the hottest of the season."

In the years since, Sean John models have regularly rocked the runway at Fashion Week shows. One of the most memorable was in February 2001, when the Sean John show was broadcast live on the E! and Style networks. It was the first-ever runway show to be nationally televised. "It is that perfect combination for us where entertainment and celebrity meets fashion and celebrity," E! president Mindy Herman told the *Los Angeles Times*. Another milestone moment for Sean John happened in 2004, when the flagship retail location opened in tandem with New York Fashion Week. Fashion icons, including Naomi Campbell, Tommy Hilfiger, and Zac Pasen, gathered to launch the new Fifth Avenue store in style with a celebratory champagne toast.

Though a hip-hop artist successfully breaking into the apparel market might seem far-fetched, expanding into fashion had been a natural progression for Combs. He'd helped mold the image of such superstars as Jodeci and Mary J. Blige. He had also carefully created an image that reflected his newfound star status. From long white furs and designer sunglasses to crisp business suits to baseball caps and baggy pants, Combs's fashion choices for himself and his artists were always daring, bold, and trendsetting.

"Music and fashion relate because both art forms are extremely passionate. They're about evolving and being forward and a certain level of creativity. They go together—you can't have one without the other," Combs has said.

On a more basic level, Combs always had a passion for fashion. As he once told Oprah, "I have rooms [for my clothes], not closets." That passion paid off in spades. In 2004, Sean John beat out fashion moguls, such as Michael Kors and Ralph Lauren, to receive the prestigious "Menswear Designer of the Year" award from the Council of Fashion Designers of America (CFDA). The award was especially gratifying as Combs had already been nominated four times but never taken home the honor. "Finally, right?" asked Combs as he danced across the stage to accept the award.

Combs's love of fashion and lifestyle also inspired him to look at it through a different lens: the pages of his own magazine, *Notorious*. After appearing on the magazine's cover when it was under different ownership, Combs had offered to buy it and relaunch it as an upscale lifestyle publication in 1998. He thought the magazine should cover everything from politics to fashion to music to business. Together with editor David Anthony, Combs crafted its new slogan: "People breaking the rules and changing the world."

Combs tapped into his impressive network to draw attention to the magazine. For the October 1999 issue, he even conducted an interview with Jennifer Lopez to capitalize on rumors about their relationship. She graced the cover clad in an angel costume. Famed musical artist Prince and Combs both appeared on other high-profile covers. However, negative headlines eventually plagued the magazine after Combs was involved with the nightclub shooting.

"Ever since the December shooting incident, advertisers are concerned that the magazine might not be right for their image," an insider told *New York* magazine. The magazine ended up ceasing publication in 2000.

Though publishing didn't pan out for Combs, the mogul had plenty of other ventures to occupy his time. Combs decided that he didn't just want the world to look good wearing his clothes and feel good listening to his music—he wanted the world to eat well, too.

In 1997, Combs had ventured into the restaurant business. He opened an upscale restaurant called Justin's (named for his son with former girlfriend Misa Hylton-Brim) in Manhattan. Among the signature dishes on the Caribbean-inspired and soul food menu were "P. Diddy's Jumbo Fried Shrimp" and "Soul Food Puffs," puffed pastries filled with jerk chicken, collard greens, rice, and peas.

The restaurant opened to great success, so much so that Combs opened another location in Atlanta's trendy Buckhead district one year later. According to *SPIN* magazine, the grand opening hosted an "army of rap and R&B stars" such as Usher and TLC, as well as players from the NFL's Atlanta Falcons. The celebrity crowd didn't waver as the years went on. The restaurant's "Martini Mondays" became a place for Atlanta's celebrities to see and be seen.

Combs saw the restaurants as opportunities to diversify his efforts and to succeed in an industry with a high turnover and failure rate. "The restaurant business is one of the riskiest businesses you can get into, but both of our restaurants are profitable," he told *Black Enterprise*.

Though Justin's far outlived many celebrity dining upstarts, Combs eventually decided to close both restaurants—New York in 2007 and Atlanta in 2012. In true "Diddy" style, Combs had simply decided to move on to other things, releasing a statement that he was pursuing "other business ventures in music, television, fashion, fragrance and spirits." He had never released sales figures for the restaurants, so it was unclear whether the decisions were purely business-based or whether Combs had just tired of the unpredictable restaurant industry.

Pursuing new ventures in television is something on which Combs has always placed a high priority. His belief in synergy between different mediums prompted him to seek ways he could promote music and artistry on the small screen. In 2002, he found a way to do that by taking over MTV's *Making the Band* franchise. The show's first incarnation had spawned hit boy band O-Town. But Combs was interested in forming a coed urban supergroup. Structured like a talent contest, the show whittled down aspiring rappers and singers until Combs chose the final six—aptly named "Da Band."

Da Band found modest success. Their album was certified gold by the RIAA, and the show lasted three seasons. However, it was the next effort of *Making the Band* that propelled Combs and his reality television stars into high ratings and widespread fame.

Combs wanted to form a megastar girl group similar to the Pussycat Dolls or Spice Girls. He threw himself into searching for his own "fab five." More than ten thousand women auditioned in a national search. Over the course of two seasons, Combs narrowed the selection down to Aubrey O'Day, Wanita

"D. Woods" Woodgett, Dawn Richard, Shannon Bex, and Aundrea Fimbres—aka Danity Kane.

The group strongly resonated with both urban and pop audiences. Their debut album *Danity Kane* reached platinum status. Danity Kane also toured as the opening act for Christina Aguilera's "Back to Basics" tour. Leapfrogging on their success, Combs continued with *Making the Band 4*.

The show chronicled their life as newfound pop stars as well as Combs's search for an equally talented boy band. The resulting group, Day26, released its first album within a week of Danity Kane's sophomore effort, *Welcome to the Dollhouse*. Both albums entered the charts at No. 1. Danity Kane became the first group in history to have two consecutive albums debut in the top spot.

On the show, Combs did double-duty in front of and behind the scenes. On-screen, he was shown working closely with the groups. The footage showed Combs giving honest feedback and critique on image, vocals, and dance ability. He often acted as everything from career coach to father figure. Combs had a tendency to be highly critical, but later admitted he may have played up his harshness to make good television: "That is reality but also some acting to make sure it's good TV. I may have pushed too hard and hurt my brand—people perceive I'm difficult to work with. This industry is life or death to me, you know? So I set a tone that lets people know how seriously I take things."

To give fans a taste of their favorite reality show in person, Combs arranged "Making the Band 4—The Tour." The tour featured Danity Kane, Day26, male solo artist Donnie Klang, and female solo artist Cheri Dennis, whose song "Ooh La La" was used as the show's theme. Though successful, the national tour proved to be the last time many of these artists would take the stage together. Danity Kane disbanded shortly afterward in a highly publicized breakup amid reports that Combs was giving Richard her own solo career. Day26 left Bad Boy Records in 2009, only to officially break up years later.

Though the bands it spawned didn't last, the *Making the Band* franchise proved successful for Combs and led to an exclusive deal with MTV for future television projects. Other MTV shows Combs has executive produced include *Run's House* (a reality show about Run DMC's Rev Run and his family); *Making His Band* (a *Making the Band* spin-off in which Combs built his own backup band); *Taquita & Kaui* (another *Making the Band* spin-off with two cast-off contestants moving to Las Vegas); *I Want to Work for Diddy* (a competition for the chance to be

Combs's assistant); and *P. Diddy's Starmaker* (an *American Idol*-style talent competition).

Through it all, Combs continued to live his lavish lifestyle in the public eye. For his twenty-ninth birthday, he threw a massive party to the tune of $600,000 at New York's luxe Cipriani Hotel. More than one thousand A-list guests attended, including Muhammad Ali, Lenny Kravitz, Donald Trump, Martha Stewart, and Mark Wahlberg.

He also began the trend of his annual "White Party," gathering many boldface names—dressed entirely in white—in the glamorous Hamptons for an unforgettable Labor Day celebration. "Puffy's always the life of the party—he makes everyone feel like they belong," Paris Hilton told *Vibe* in 2006.

Combs once recalled the inaugural White Party as the favorite event he's ever thrown. "I wanted to strip away everyone's image and put us all in the same color and on the same level," he said. "I had the craziest mix: some of my boys from Harlem [and] Leonardo DiCaprio, after he'd just finished *Titanic*. I had socialites there and relatives from down south. There were 200 people sitting out here, just having a down-home cookout. It lasted until the next morning."

Combs has held his legendary White Party annually ever since. Locations have ranged from the Hamptons to Los Angeles to France's glamorous

Saint-Tropez. Though expensive decoration, great music, and inviting style are all a given, it's the laundry list of major celebrities in attendance that makes it "the" desirable invite of choice among Hollywood circles. Yet for Combs, it's the diverse mix of people that truly makes it memorable. "My life has been about breaking down barriers. In the Hamptons, I'm just being myself. I don't act different with [billionaire] Ron Perelman than I act with Russell Simmons. I don't act different with Busta Rhymes than I act with Donald Trump. I act the same way I act," Combs told the *New York Observer* in 2006. "I'm just Puff."

Over the years, birthdays have continued to provide a good excuse for Combs to get his party planner on. For his fortieth birthday in 2009, Combs threw a $3 million black-tie affair to remember at the famed Plaza Hotel in New York. With a motif that MTV called "Garden of Eden meets 'The Godfather,'" the lavish party featured ballerinas serving drinks, giant black chandeliers, and real apples hanging from the trees. Guests as varied as Andre Harrell, Reverend Al Sharpton, Martha Stewart, Bono, Kim Kardashian, and rappers Nelly and Jay-Z mixed and mingled to celebrate their favorite hip-hop superstar.

"Some people start at 19, [and by] 26, they're done. He's 40. He's better than he's ever been," Russell Simmons told MTV. "He's hotter now than ever. . . .

He keeps getting better. He never changes with the hustle. He branches out in different areas, opens new doors. He's an inspiration."

The party planning didn't stop that year for Combs, as his son Justin turned sixteen just two months later. And what better way to celebrate than with a "super-sized Sweet 16 party" featured on MTV. Held at the M2 Ultralounge in New York on January 23, 2010, the party featured performances from such rappers as Nicki Minaj and Fabolous. Perhaps most memorable, though, was the gift from father to son: the keys to a $360,000 silver Maybach car. Combs also gave Justin a check for $10,000, which he donated to help victims of a devastating earthquake that had happened in Haiti just weeks earlier.

Combs's reputation for having great taste and enjoying the good life has earned him several major brand endorsements. In 2005, Combs appeared in a memorable Diet Pepsi commercial aired during the Super Bowl. In the commercial, he arrives to an awards show in a Diet Pepsi truck and sparks a new trend. That year, Combs also endorsed skin-care solution Proactiv. He appeared in an infomercial about the wonders it had worked for his own skin. "Diddy's not a celeb who'd ever be thought of as 'selling out,'" Proactiv guru Guthy Renker told *Forbes*.

"When we signed P. Diddy, we saw a shift in the way we were perceived."

In 2006, Combs joined forces with Burger King to launch *Diddy TV*. The branded YouTube channel showed videos designed to give viewers a glimpse into Combs's personal life. The venture coincided with the release of Combs's album *Press Play*. "I'm having it my way on this album, and it's been a great journey for me, so I'm grateful for partners like Burger King Corporation that are helping me bring a fresh sound to my fans," Combs said in a statement. "They share my passion for being tastemakers and giving the people what they want."

Perhaps the most high-profile of Combs's endorsements was the 2007 deal he signed with Ciroc Vodka to become its brand ambassador and an equal-share owner. Calling himself "Ciroc Obama," Combs has become a promoter for the brand. He creates custom "Diddy" cocktails, shows the vodka off in music videos, promotes the brand via social media, and appears in commercials and billboard ads. The tactics have worked. *Forbes* reported that sales had skyrocketed from 120,000 cases sold in 2007 to more than one million in 2011. The article even predicted that the Ciroc partnership could eventually make Combs "hip-hop's first billionaire."

Whether he hits the billionaire mark or not, Combs has cemented himself among business circles as a big-picture thinker and savvy businessman. Both a risk-taker and an influencer, Combs is always in motion—and that's just how he prefers it. "I tell people all the time, when they ask about me being relentless, that if you tie me up and drop me in the middle of the desert with no water, no clothes, I'm going to come out of that desert with a Sean John three-piece suit on, sipping a Ciroc martini," Combs told CNBC in 2007. "I'm not going to stop."

Chapter 7

BEEN AROUND THE WORLD

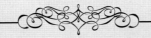

N ot all freshman football players have their first collegiate game filmed and featured on the *Diddy TV* YouTube channel. But then again, not all college freshmen are Justin Dior Combs. When Justin took the field at Pasadena's Rose Bowl for the UCLA Bruins' first game of the 2012–2013 season versus the Nebraska Cornhuskers, Sean Combs was every part the proud papa. "This feeling of your child accomplishing something that they work hard for, that you instilled in them as parents—it can't be expressed in words," Combs shared in a 2012 YouTube video.

For Combs, who had long ago dreamed of being a professional football player himself, the moment was especially meaningful. He had never lost his love of football, and earlier that year, he executive produced a documentary titled *Undefeated*. The film followed a year in the life of the football team at Manassas High School in Memphis, Tennessee. Viewers were able to see the impact that its inspiring coach was able to make on its players.

Combs had gotten involved after being approached by the coach of his son's Little League team. "He called me and said, 'I've got something special. It's not for business or for money. It's for art.' I saw it and it just blew me away," he told the *New York Times* in 2012. "You think it's going to be about football, but it's about life. I just related to it in so many ways." Audiences and critics agreed, and in February 2012, *Undefeated* won the Academy Award for "Best Documentary."

Looking ahead, Combs has said he wants to see his son Justin playing football professionally. It's clear that his dreams for all of his children are as far-reaching as his own. To date, Combs has five biological children: Justin (born in 1993 to Misa Hylton-Brim); Christian (born in 1998 to Kim Porter); twins D'Lila Star and Jessie James (born in 2006 to Porter); and Chance (born in 2006 to mother Sarah Chapman).

Combs also acts as a surrogate stepfather to Porter's son Quincy.

To date, Christian and Justin have modeled for Sean John, while Chance has modeled for the Belk catalog. Both Quincy and Justin have appeared on MTV's *My Super Sweet 16*. In 2012, all of Combs's kids banded together to record a special birthday song written by Quincy for Combs. The entertainment gene runs in the family—Porter even goes as far as to call Christian his father's clone, saying, "He dances like Puffy. He's very driven like him and very focused. It's amazing, the DNA. He is absolutely 100 percent just like his father."

But while Combs is proud at the prospect of his children following in his footsteps, he's most gratified by the family time they get to spend together. "I feel truly blessed and appreciative just to be able to wake up this morning and be able to see my kids," Combs told *Ebony* in 2001. "For the longest time, I focused on really being the greatest entertainer and entrepreneur that I could be. This makes you evaluate to make sure that you can be the best person that you can be, the best father. God and my family are first in my life."

With three different mothers to his children and an array of other "leading ladies" in his life, Combs has certainly led a colorful romantic past. His first love was Hylton-Brim. Combs had courted her through his early days at Uptown Records. She had seen him through tough times, such as the City College basketball scandal. They'd broken up while Hylton-Brim was pregnant with Justin. Looking back, Combs blamed his hyper-focus on career. "I was busy, and having a family wasn't my priority. She deserved to have what she wanted out of life."[1]

Around that time, Combs began dating fashion model Kim Porter. They'd met while she was working at Uptown Records as a receptionist. The two entered into an "on-again, off-again" relationship that lasted for more than a decade. Both admit it wasn't always easy. One of the low points was Combs's relationship with Jennifer Lopez shortly after Christian was born.

"I never thought it was real," Porter said to *OK! Magazine* in 2007. "Despite what you see in print and when the cameras are flashing, what's going on in someone's heart may be totally different. He was still in love with me. I never looked at their relationship as serious."

Another low point for the pair was the secret relationship Combs allegedly carried on with Sarah Chapman while he was still with Porter, resulting in his daughter Chance being born the same year that Porter gave birth to twins. Combs requested DNA tests to prove that Chapman's daughter was his own.

Once that was proven, Combs pledged to "take care of her for the rest of her life."

However, the damage was done with Porter. The two broke up for good in 2007. They do maintain a strong friendship, however, and even vacationed with their children together in St. Bart's in 2010. "You know how when two people go their separate ways, most of the time there's animosity? It's not like that with us," Porter told *Essence.* "Sean and I have this bond, this friendship. . . . I'm the person he can tell his innermost thoughts to, and he's that person for me. He still calls me every day and we talk."

Combs was equally appreciative of Porter. "I ain't gonna lie: I'm hard to love," Combs told *Vibe* in 2006. "My hat goes off to her or anybody else who's dealt with me, because a lot of [my] time and attention is really not on that person. A woman deserves to be nurtured and taken care of. Kim taught me that. She . . . taught me how to love."

Currently, Combs is rumored to be in a serious relationship with Cassie Ventura, aka "Cassie." Cassie is a Bad Boy recording artist and one-time model. Though they were coy about whether they were dating for many years, the couple sent out Twitter messages in September 2012 confessing their love for each other. They also attended a Halloween party together at the Playboy Mansion one month later.

The pair has recorded several songs together, including one titled "Must Be Love."

The ups and downs of Combs's private life have provided plenty of professional inspiration reflected in his music. Though his life hasn't always been easy, his array of experiences has resulted in a vault of endless material. "So much has happened to me. I dare you to write it all down, to go through every dramatic point in my life," Combs said to CNBC in 2007. "It's scary: my father, the City College situation, Biggie's death, the death of my two best friends, running a marathon, winning a Grammy, selling out Madison Square Garden. It's a lot to digest. It's five lives in one."

When *Press Play* came out in 2006, Combs said that many of the songs were based on his relationships with Lopez and Porter. He called the album his "most personal record" yet. "On a lot of the other records, to be honest, I didn't do a whole lot of writing; on this one, I did a lot," Combs admitted. "And I exposed myself with everybody's most sensitive subject, and that's the subject of love."[2]

With the 2010 release of Combs's most recent album, *Last Train to Paris,* he continued to draw from experience and explore more personal themes and feelings. Most notably, the hit song "Coming Home" addressed his fear of not being the right kind of role model for his children. The lyrics included personal revelations about marriage and family life. Combs also openly talked about how he'll answer hard questions from his children about his life choices.

"I am going to show the world a refreshing new side of me. [The album] is deeper than any other stuff I have ever made. It's a profound love story," Combs told *AceShowbiz.com* in 2009. "I've been a businessman for the past two years. It's time for me to focus on being an artist again."

The gamble paid off. *Entertainment Weekly* called the album "his best work in years."

While Combs acknowledges that he's not perfect, he has made many efforts to be a strong role model for both his family and fans as an active philanthropist. For Combs, it seems the old adage "Charity starts at home" holds true. Many of his philanthropic efforts have benefited places that are personally meaningful to him.

In 1999, Combs donated $500,000 to Howard University in order to establish the Sean Combs and Janice Combs Scholarship Fund. Combs presented the check at a dinner of 1,700 guests. The donation marked the most money ever given to Howard University by one individual. Its designated purpose was to create scholarships for students pursuing careers in the entertainment business.

His hometown of Harlem is another area where Combs has concentrated his efforts. When its Boys & Girls Club was in danger of going out of business, Combs donated $60,000 to keep it running. The donation helped sustain basketball games, math and reading tutors, and gym classes for more than three thousand kids across four different Harlem locations. "Being from Harlem, I heard they needed help and I wanted to help," Combs said to the *New York Daily News* in 2011. "This is something that I am proud to do."

Combs also sought to make a long-term impact on his former community. From 1994 to 2007, he spearheaded Daddy's House Social Programs. This nonprofit organization was geared at providing educational opportunities and programming for disadvantaged youth. The organization operated out of the Harlem YMCA and was run by hip-hop activist Sister Souljah. Special initiatives included a course on economics and stock trading with a Wall Street firm and an international travel group that took ten to fifteen students on an annual trip to places such as South Africa. Daddy's House Social Programs also fed more than one thousand homeless families in Harlem every Thanksgiving.

"Our goal is to help young people prepare for today's world by giving them hope and direction,"

Combs told the *Los Angeles Times* in 1999. "I want to provide opportunities for those who [are] not as fortunate as I was."

Though Daddy's House Social Programs ended in 2007, Combs hasn't stopped his efforts to further the education of Harlem's youth. In 2010, Combs announced plans to open a business school in Harlem during an interview on CNN. "I want to have an academy that is known for building leaders," Combs said. "I feel that's one of the things I can have an impact on."

Combs has also used his position of influence to help raise money for worthy causes. In 2003, he decided to run the New York City Marathon. His goal was not only to challenge himself, but also to raise at least one million dollars to be divided between Children's Hope Foundation, his own Daddy's House Social Programs, and the public schools of New York City. Combs knew it would be an uphill battle to prepare for the 26.2-mile run.

"I run one mile, I'm ready to pass out and go to bed for the week," he confessed. "A marathon is one of the most physically and mentally challenging things you can do, so I came up with this crazy idea to run the marathon."[3]

Combs went the distance—finishing in just over four hours and raising more than 2 million dollars.

He doubled his fund-raising goal with the help of some of his famous friends, such as Ben Affleck (who donated $52,000), Jennifer Lopez (who gave $26,000), and Jay-Z (who gave $25,000). For Combs, the experience was rewarding on a number of levels and reflected some of his life's philosophies. "I kind of feel sometimes like my life is a marathon," Combs said to *NY1.com* in 2003. "There have been a lot of ups and downs, good times and bad times—but really, it's about how you finish."

The political sphere is another area where Combs wanted to make an impact. For the 2004 presidential election, Combs partnered with MTV's Rock the Vote campaign designed to generate more interest among young Americans ages eighteen to thirty. He also created his own campaign known as Citizen Change, specifically aimed at Latino and African-American youths. Combs's goal? "To make voting cool."

The campaign spearheaded widespread outreach efforts. T-shirts were created with such slogans as "Vote or Die." Combs got former presidential adviser James Carville to lend his expertise. Celebrities, such as Leonardo DiCaprio, Mariah Carey, and Mary J. Blige, did their part, too. "This is not just about talk, this is about action. The forgotten ones, the over 40 million minorities and young people, will decide who will be President of the United States. And I have the numbers to prove it," Combs said at New York University. "The last election was decided by just 537 votes. We will make a difference. You do the math." Combs's comments were especially relevant in light of the heated race between George W. Bush and Al Gore four years earlier, in which a recount had been necessary to determine the final result.

Combs also worked the election circuit in 2008 and 2012. He was a strong advocate for Democratic candidate Barack Obama. Having interviewed Obama in an exclusive YouTube video during the 2004 election, Combs went on to appear at several Obama rallies. Two days before the 2012 election, Combs tweeted on his birthday that all he wanted as a present was a victory for Obama.

"I think [the hip-hop community is] probably responsible for Obama being in office . . . the confidence, the swagger we instilled in our communities made that possible," Combs said in a *Playboy* interview in 2009. "I ain't gonna lie—if God said I could pick one person to be my father, I'd want to be Sean Combs Obama. That's how dope he is."

Combs may not be running for president himself anytime soon, but he has no plans on halting his quest for world—or at least industry—domination. In late 2012, he partnered with Macy's to launch an innovative clothing line featuring built-in video screens. Plans are in the works for Combs to debut his own cable channel, Revolt, which will be a social media-driven music and news television channel. Combs is also slated to appear in the upcoming action movie *Shoedog,* costarring Heather Graham and country star Kris Kristofferson. Whether it's in music, business, fashion, politics, or another arena, Combs's ultimate goal is simple: "To make history."

Yet the legacy Combs wants to leave is not necessarily a catalog of hip-hop hits or a billionaire bank account. Rather, Combs aims to change the way urban youths are viewed and to help them maximize their potential. "[To me, making history means] having people look at people in a different way," Combs has said. "The next time a young black kid with his hat turned to the back walks into an office, he may just be looked at in a different way because of Puff Daddy."[4]

And *that* is exactly what makes Combs an African-American icon.

CHRONOLOGY

1969—Sean John Combs is born to Melvin and Janice Combs on November 4.

1982—Janice Combs relocates the family from Harlem to Mount Vernon.

1988—Combs enters Howard University as a freshman.

1993—Combs is promoted to vice president of Artists & Repertoire at Uptown Records.

1997—Christopher Wallace, aka "the Notorious B.I.G," is shot and killed following the Soul Train Awards in Los Angeles. Months later, Combs releases his debut album *No Way Out* featuring a tribute song to Wallace.

1999—Combs appears on the cover of *Forbes* alongside comedian Jerry Seinfeld for its "Celebrity 100" issue.

2002—Combs appears in the Broadway revival of *A Raisin in the Sun*, which receives a Tony Award nomination.

2004—Sean John opens its first flagship store in New York City; Combs performs during the halftime show of Super Bowl XXXVIII alongside stars Janet Jackson, Justin Timberlake, Kid Rock, and Jessica Simpson.

2005—Combs sells a 50 percent stake in Bad Boy to Warner Music for $30 million.

2006—Combs's first fragrance, Unforgivable, is released, and it sells more than $150 million its first year; Chicago Mayor Richard M. Daley names October 13 "Diddy Day" to commemorate Combs's charitable contributions.

2008—Combs gets a star on the Hollywood Walk of Fame.

2012—Combs is named "Hip-Hop's Wealthiest Artist" by *Forbes* with an estimated net worth of $550 million.

Discography & Filmography

Selected Filmography

Made (2001)

Monster's Ball (2001)

Death of a Dynasty (2003)

A Raisin in the Sun (TV movie, 2008)

Get Him to the Greek (2010)

Shoedog (2014)

Selected Discography

No Way Out (1997)

Forever (1999)

The Saga Continues . . . (2001)

We Invented the Remix (2002)

Press Play (2006)

Last Train to Paris (2010)

Selected Awards

Songwriter of the Year, American Society of Composers and Publishers, 1996

Man of the Year, *XXL Magazine,* 1997

Howard University Alumni Award for Distinguished Postgraduate Achievement, 1999

Style Maverick Award, *Vibe* Awards, 2003

Menswear Designer of the Year, Council of Fashion Designers of America, 2004

100 Most Influential People, *Time,* 2006

NAACP Image Award for Outstanding Actor, 2009

Founders Award, American Society of Composers and Publishers, 2011

Triumph Award, National Action Network, 2012

Forbes Celebrity 100, 2009–2012

CHAPTER NOTES

Chapter 1: The Father of Reinvention

1. "Sean Combs: Monster's Ball," *BravoTV.com*, n.d., <http://www.bravotv.com/inside-the-actors-studio/videos/sean-combs-monsters-ball> (February 28, 2013).

2. "Sean Combs: Transcript," *CNBC.com*, November 7, 2007, <http://www.cnbc.com/id/25059077/> (February 28, 2013).

Chapter 2: Growing Up Diddy

1. Ronin Ro, *Bad Boy: The Influence of Sean "Puffy" Combs on the Music Industry* (New York: Pocket Books, 2001), Kindle edition, Chapter 1.

2. "One On 1: Hip-Hop Mogul Sean 'P. Diddy' Combs," *NY1.com*, October 27, 2003, <http://www.ny1.com/content/features/one_on_1_archives/one_on__1_cmco/34269/one-on-1--hip-hop-mogul-sean--p--diddy--combs> (December 15, 2012).

3. "Oprah Interviews Sean Combs," *Oprah.com*, November 2006, <http://www.oprah.com/omagazine/Oprah-Interviews-Sean-Combs-P-Diddy-Puff-Daddy/2> (December 1, 2012).

4. Ro, Chapter 1.

5. "Puff Daddy to Invade Indianapolis," *Indiana.edu*, 1997, <http://www.indiana.edu/~ids/archives/1114pdaddy.html> (November 18, 2012).

Chapter 3: Hip-Hop's Newest Bad Boy

1. Ronin Ro, *Bad Boy: The Influence of Sean "Puffy" Combs on the Music Industry* (New York: Pocket Books, 2001), Kindle edition, Chapter 1.

2. "Disrespecting the Bling," *CityPaper.com*, April 25, 2001, <http://www2.citypaper.com/music/story.asp?id=8299> (March 1, 2013).

3. Ro, Chapter 1.

Chapter 4: Thinking B.I.G.

1. "Bad Boy, Vibe 1999," *DreamHamptonArticles.blogspot.com*, December 30, 1991, <http://dreamhamptonarticles.blogspot.com/2010/04/bad-boy-vibe-history-of-hip-hop.html> (November 15, 2012).

2. "Andre Harell on the Legend of Diddy," *YouTube.com*, July 22, 2010, <https://www.youtube.com/watch?v=hRmvA1Hf4HA> (March 1, 2013).

3. Ronin Ro, *Bad Boy: The Influence of Sean "Puffy" Combs on the Music Industry* (New York: Pocket Books, 2001), Kindle edition, Chapter 3.

4. Ibid.

Chapter 5: Suddenly in the Spotlight

1. Jake Brown, *Ready to Die: The Story of Biggie Smalls* (London: Amber Books Publishing, 2004), p. 96.

Chapter 6: More Than Music

1. Ronin Ro, *Bad Boy: The Influence of Sean "Puffy" Combs on the Music Industry* (New York: Pocket Books, 2001), Kindle edition, Chapter 1.

Chapter 7: Been Around the World

1. Ronin Ro, *Bad Boy: The Influence of Sean "Puffy" Combs on the Music Industry* (New York: Pocket Books, 2001), Kindle edition, Chapter 3.

2. "Diddy Talks About J.Lo On His New Album," *People.com*, October 9, 2006, <http://www.people.com/people/article/0,,1544027,00.html> (February 28, 2013).

3. "Diddy Runs the City," *Vimeo.com*, March 2012, <http://vimeo.com/35295537> (February 28, 2013).

4. "Puff Daddy's Black & White Ball '98," *Observer.com*, December 4, 2006, <http://observer.com/2006/12/puff-daddys-black-and-white-ball-98/> (March 1, 2013).

GLOSSARY

acclaim—High praise.

allegations—A statement or accusation made without concrete proof.

audacity—Boldly disrespectful behavior.

capitalize—To take advantage of.

cerebral palsy—A disability resulting from damage to the brain before, during, or shortly after birth and outwardly manifested by muscular incoordination and speech disturbances.

entourage—A group of people that surround and support one specific person.

entrepreneur—Someone who runs a business.

explicit—Containing inappropriate or adult content.

fruition—Realization.

"Ghetto Fabulous"—An urban term used to symbolize wealth and glamour.

improvisation—To make, invent, or arrange offhand.

liability—Legal responsibility.

persona—Someone's public image or personality.

philanthropic—Charitable or beneficial to a cause or group.

synergy—The way two things work together to create a greater effect.

FURTHER READING

Books

Gelfand, Dale Evva. *Sean Combs*. New York: Chelsea House, 2007.

Traugh, Susan M. *Sean Combs*. Detroit: Lucent Books, 2010.

Wittmann, Kelly. *Sean "Diddy" Combs*. Broomall, Pa.: Mason Crest Publishers, 2007.

Wolny, Philip. *Sean Combs*. New York: Rosen Publishing Group, 2006.

Internet Addresses

Biography.com: Sean "Puffy" Combs
<http://www.biography.com/people/sean-puffy-combs-9542180>

Forbes.com: Sean "Diddy" Combs
<http://www.forbes.com/profile/sean-diddy-combs/>

INDEX